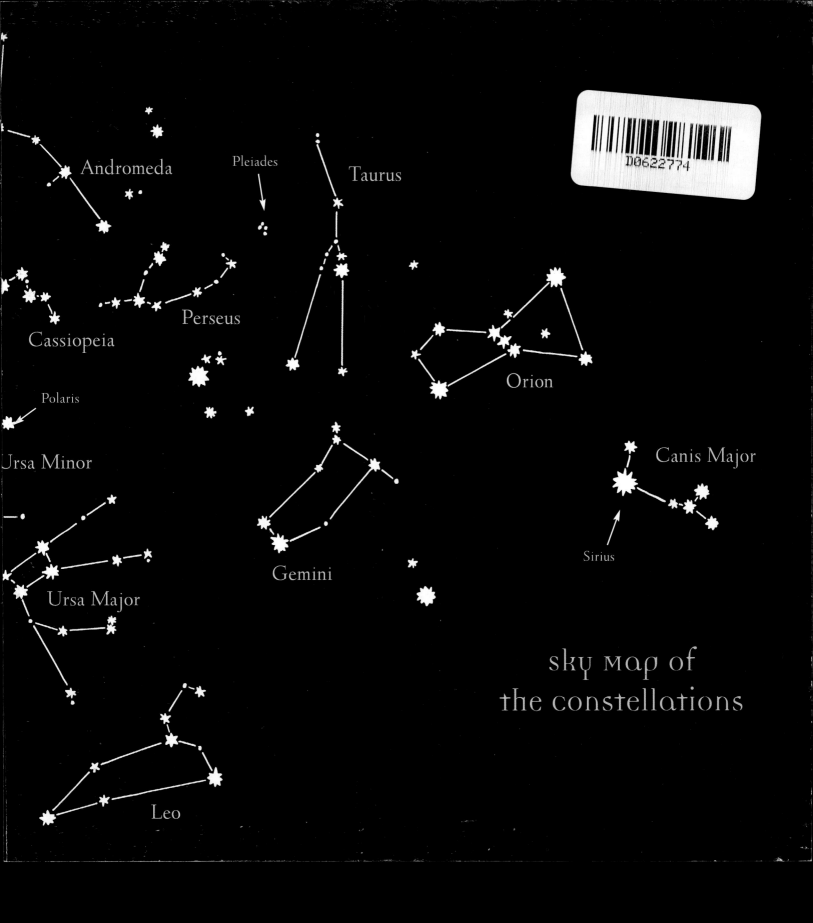

Andromeda

Pleiades

Taurus

Cassiopeia

Perseus

Polaris

Orion

Ursa Minor

Canis Major

Gemini

Sirius

Ursa Major

Leo

sky map of
the constellations

constellations

A Glow-in-the-Dark Guide to the Night Sky

To my nieces Danielle, Marielle, and Sydney—who always glow.

—C.S.

ABOUT THE ILLUSTRATOR

Alan Flinn has been illustrating children's books for over twenty years, including *Elliott Finds a Clue* and *Elliott's Talking Dog*. He lives in Colorado Springs, CO.

Library of Congress Cataloging-in-Publication Data

Sasaki, Chris.
Constellations : a glow-in-the-dark guide to the night sky / Chris Sasaki ; illustrated by Alan Flinn.
p. cm.
Includes index.
ISBN 1-4027-0385-6
1. Constellations—Juvenile literature.   I. Flinn, Alan, ill. II. Title.
QB802.S27 2006
523.8—dc22
2005023280

2 4 6 8 10 9 7 5 3

Published by Sterling Publishing Co., Inc.
387 Park Avenue South, New York, NY 10016
Text ©2006 by Chris Sasaki
Illustrations ©2006 by Alan Flinn
Distributed in Canada by Sterling Publishing
% Canadian Manda Group, 165 Dufferin Street
Toronto, Ontario, Canada M6K 3H6
Distributed in Great Britain and Europe by Chris Lloyd at Orca Book
Services, Stanley House, Fleets Lane, Poole BH15 3AJ, England
Distributed in Australia by Capricorn Link (Australia) Pty. Ltd.
P.O. Box 704, Windsor, NSW 2756, Australia

Sterling ISBN-13:978-1-4027-0385-0
ISBN-10:1-4027-0385-6

For information about custom editions, special sales, premium and
corporate purchases, please contact Sterling Special Sales
Department at 800-805-5489 or specialsales@sterlingpub.com.

constellations

A Glow-in-the-Dark Guide to the Night Sky

by chris sasaki illustrated by Alan flinn

Sterling Publishing Co., Inc.
New York

stories in the stars

It's a clear dark night. Look up! What do you see? If you are outside, far from city lights, you see thousands of stars. When you look up do you see different shapes made of stars? Can you see triangles? Squares and curved lines? Can you imagine pictures made of stars?

For thousands of years, people have looked up at the night sky and seen star pictures. Some of the star pictures look like mythic heroes or gods. Others look like animals or imaginary creatures. Today, we call those star pictures constellations.

Look at a star map. Many of the constellations are named after the gods, heroes, and creatures from Greek myths. But other people see star pictures of caribou and foxes, or bears, birds, and forest animals. They look into the sky and see things that are important to them.

Some of the constellations were named by scientists who studied the star patterns. In all, 88 constellations cover the sky like a giant jigsaw puzzle. The constellations make the night sky the biggest storybook ever. It is there for you to read—every clear, dark night.

ursa major, the great bear

A great bear looks down from the night sky. It is called Ursa Major. Stars make up the bear's head, body and legs. Seven bright stars in the bear look like a big pot with a long handle. We call it the Big Dipper.

There are many stories about Ursa Major. In one, a goddess named Callisto was turned into a bear. One day, her son saw the bear and followed it, not knowing he was hunting his own mother. Before she could be shot, Callisto was placed in the night sky, safe from her son's arrows.

Many years ago, slaves in the southern United States looked at the Big Dipper and saw a drinking gourd, hollowed out to carry water. The slaves sang a song called "Follow the Drinking Gourd." The song told them that if they followed the stars north, they would find freedom—and they did.

ursa minor, the Bear cub

Imagine standing on the North Pole. If you looked straight up, you would see a bright star. It is the most famous star of all. It is called Polaris, or the North Star.

The North Star is the brightest star in Ursa Minor, the Little Bear. Ursa Minor is also called the Little Dipper. The North Star and two other stars make the dipper's handle. Four stars make the bowl of the dipper.

Even if you're not at the North Pole, it's easy to find the North Star. First, find the Big Dipper. Pretend there is a line from the two outer stars in the bowl of the Big Dipper. That line points right to the North Star. This star is special. When you turn and face it, you are facing north. It's like a compass in the sky!

Draco, the Dragon

The stars of Draco the Dragon curl around Ursa Minor and the North Star. It looks like the dragon is guarding the North Star.

In a story from long ago, Draco guarded a very special apple tree. The tree was a gift to the greatest of the Greek gods, Hera and Zeus. It was a very special gift because the apples that hung from its branches were made of gold. The gods did not want anyone stealing their precious apples, so they had the dragon guard the tree. It worked. Draco kept everyone away, except the great hero, Hercules. With his strength and courage, Hercules fought the beast and picked the golden fruit.

cassiopeia, the queen

Five bright stars shine like a glimmering letter "W" in the northern night sky. Use your imagination and look at these stars. Can you see a queen sitting on a throne? Her name is Cassiopeia.

Queen Cassiopeia liked looking at herself in the mirror. She thought she was beautiful. This made the gods angry, so the god of the sea sent a monster to attack Cassiopeia's kingdom.

What else do you see in the five stars of Cassiopeia? The Inuit, who live in the Arctic, believed that the stars looked like steps cut into the snow. By climbing the steps you could reach the sky. Other North American natives imagined an elk skin stretched across the sky. The elk skin was so large, it could be hung only in the heavens. The five stars were holes in the elk hide, made by wooden stakes that pinned it to the sky.

orion, the hunter

Orion the Hunter stands like a giant in the winter night sky. Two bright stars shine from his shoulders. Two more adorn his legs. His belt is made up of a row of stars. Look carefully and you'll see the stars in his club and shield, too.

Orion gazes toward a group of stars called the Pleiades. The Pleiades were seven beautiful sisters. Orion fell in love with them, but the seven sisters weren't interested. Every night, Orion follows them through the sky, but can never catch them.

The Inuit see a different picture. To them, the star in Orion's right shoulder is a polar bear. The stars of Orion's belt are hunters following the bear. Just as Orion never catches the Pleiades, these hunters never catch the bear.

Taurus, the Bull

Do you see a group of stars in the winter night sky shaped like the letter V? This is the face of Taurus, the Bull. The bull glares down from above with bright stars for eyes. Two stars shine from the sharp tips of the bull's horns.

A small cluster of stars sits on the bull's shoulder. These are the Pleiades. To the Iroquois, these stars were young boys who spent their days dancing. One day, the boys danced and danced, until they began to rise into the air. Higher and higher they flew. They rose far up into the heavens and became the star cluster we see today.

andromeda, the princess

The constellation of Princess Andromeda lies in the autumn night sky. It looks like a long arc of stars. But the princess is not happy. On star maps, you can see that she is chained to a rock!

Poseidon was angry with Andromeda's mother, Cassiopeia, and sent the sea monster Cetus to attack the Queen's kingdom. There was only one way to stop the monster from ravaging the land. King Cepheus chained his own daughter to the rocky shore. The King hoped the monster would find his daughter and spare the kingdom.

Does this story have a happy ending? You'll find out when you read about Perseus.

perseus, the hero

In the autumn night sky, look for a crooked V of stars not far from Andromeda. That's the hero Perseus.

Perseus was a great warrior. He even defeated Medusa, whose head was covered with serpents. She was so hideous, one look at her would turn you to stone. When Perseus fought Medusa, he used his shiny shield as a mirror. By looking at Medusa's reflection instead, Perseus was able to kill her and cut off her head without turning to stone.

After the battle with Medusa, Perseus happened upon Princess Andromeda. She had been chained to some rocks and was being attacked by a sea monster. Perseus came to Andromeda's rescue. He held up Medusa's head before the creature. The monster took one look, turned to stone, and sank beneath the waves. Andromeda was saved!

pegasus, the winged horse

Pegasus, the winged horse, flies through autumn night skies. Do you see four stars that form a large square? The square is the horse's body. Other stars mark the front legs and head of this beautiful animal.

Pegasus was a wild creature. Only the young Greek Prince Bellerophon could ride him, using a bridle made of gold. Together, the two set out to battle the Chimera, a beast that was part goat, lion, and serpent, and breathed fire. Still, the Chimera was no match for Bellerophon and Pegasus. The two soared down from the sky and defeated the three-headed monster.

cygnus, the swan

Look up on a clear summer night, and you'll see Cygnus the Swan soaring along the Milky Way. Bright stars form the body, wings, neck and head of the beautiful bird.

To some native people, Cygnus is a snow goose. One day, the goose was gliding along the surface of a lake, when three hunters saw it and took aim. The startled goose took flight, but it was too late. The great bird fell into the water.

The hunters paddled onto the lake in their canoe, searching for the snow goose. The sky grew dark. Stars appeared and were reflected in the water. The hunters looked up. The snow goose had become a constellation, soaring through the night sky.

Aquila, The Eagle

The constellation Aquila is an eagle that flies through the summer night sky. Aquila's brightest star is Altair.

In a story told in Japan and China, Vega was the Sun God's daughter. Altair was the young man who took care of the Sun God's cattle. The two fell in love, but as their love grew, they forgot their work. The Sun God became angry and sent Altair to the far side of the river of the Milky Way.

Vega went to the magpies for help. That is why, each year on the seventh day of the seventh month, the birds fly up and form a bridge across the Milky Way. Altair and Vega meet on this bridge of wings and shed happy tears at seeing each other again.

Hercules

It's summer. Look straight up. Do you see stars that look like a crooked H? You are looking at Hercules, one of the greatest heroes in the sky. The H is the body of Hercules. Other stars make up the hero's head, arms, and legs. He's even holding a club.

Hercules was the strongest man who ever lived. He became a god by performing twelve tasks, including battling a lion with his bare hands. That lion is now the constellation Leo the Lion.

The sky is full of other creatures Hercules fought. He battled Hydra, the serpent with a hundred heads, and Cancer the Crab. He hunted Cygnus the Swan and Aquila the Eagle. The great hero even fought and beat Draco the Dragon. Look up in the night sky and you'll see him there—standing over the defeated dragon.

leo, the lion

Can you find Leo, the Lion? Look for a backwards question mark below the bowl of the Big Dipper. That's the lion's mane. A triangle of stars is the lion's hindquarters and tail. The dot of the question mark is a bright star called Regulus, which means "little king." The brightest star of the triangle is called Denebola, which means "lion's tail."

The Greeks looked at Leo and saw the fierce lion killed by Hercules. But other people saw different animals in these stars. The Incas of Peru saw a big cat called a puma. And the Chinese saw a horse. Can you see any other animals in the stars of Leo?

gemini, the twins

Not far from Orion the Hunter are the Gemini Twins. The bright star Castor is the head of one twin. And the shining star Pollux is the head of the other.

In Greek myths, Castor and Pollux were the sons of Zeus. They were great warriors who sailed with Jason and the Argonauts aboard their ship the Argo. Once, Jason and his crew were trapped on an island with a giant who could kill his opponents with a single blow. The giant challenged the sailors of the Argo to a boxing match. But only Pollux was brave enough to accept the challenge. With skill and speed, Pollux defeated the giant, freeing the Argonauts to set sail again.

Lyra, The Harp

The night sky is filled with heroes, animals and strange creatures. There is also a musical instrument in the stars. It is Lyra, Orpheus' Harp. Lyra looks like a small triangle and a slanted rectangle made of stars.

Along with Castor and Pollux, Orpheus sailed with the Argonauts. One day, the Argo and its crew were passing an island where the Sirens lived. The Sirens were sea demons whose songs lured sailors to their deaths. The Argonauts could not resist steering toward the sound, so Orpheus took up his harp and began to sing. At the beautiful sound of this music, the sailors stopped listening to the demons and steered to safety. Orpheus and his harp had saved the ship.

Boötes, the Bear Driver

Every night, Boötes the Bear Driver follows Ursa Major across the sky. To the Micmac, who live on the east coast of Canada, the stars of Boötes are hunters who also chase the bear.

The Micmac say that one spring, a bear woke up and left its cave. It was spotted by Chickadee, a bird who quickly called his friends to join in the hunt. They chased the bear until autumn, when the tired bear could run no more.

Robin shot the bear with an arrow, and drops of blood spattered on Robin's feathers and the forest leaves. The birds killed the bear, but its spirit was strong and it is reborn each spring. To the Micmac, this is why robins have red breasts and why leaves turn red in the fall. And, it's why we still see the hunters chasing the bear every night.

canis major, the greater dog

Canis Major is one of Orion's hunting dogs, running through the winter night sky. It doesn't look much like a dog, but it's easy to find. Imagine a line through Orion's belt. Follow it and you'll come to Sirius, the brightest star in Canis Major and the brightest star in the night sky. Look carefully at Sirius. Does it twinkle, or sparkle with different colors?

The Inuit of the eastern Arctic call the star Singuuriq. That means "flickering." To them, Sirius is the flame of an old woman's seal-oil lamp, flickering in the breeze from her window.

Inuit who live in the western Arctic call the star Kajuqtuq Tiriganniarlu. That means "red fox and white fox." When they look at Sirius, they see two foxes fighting to get into the same hole. The star changes color because one fox is white and one is red.

sagittarius, the archer

Sagittarius is a strange archer. He is half man and half horse, riding through the summer night sky. It's no wonder he is holding a bow and arrow. To the Greeks, the archer is named Crotus. And it was Crotus who invented archery!

To most people, the eight bright stars of Sagittarius look more like a teapot with a handle, a lid and a top. There are also six stars close by that look like a teaspoon. Look closely and you'll see other stars that look like a slice of lemon. You're all ready for a tea party!

scorpius, the scorpion

To the Greeks, a long line of stars form the giant scorpion named Scorpius. But to the Maori of New Zealand, the stars are a magic fish hook.

The fish hook belonged to a young boy named Maui. One day, Maui hid in his brothers' fishing canoe. When the brothers found Maui, they were very angry. They let him stay, but they wouldn't give him a hook or bait.

So, Maui took out a magic jawbone and used it as a hook. The young boy soon caught a huge fish and pulled it into the canoe. Suddenly the fish turned to stone, fell back into the ocean, and became islands. Maui tossed the magic hook into the sky. And, it's still there for you to see—in the stars of Scorpius.

A constellation of activities

invent a new constellation

YOU'LL NEED:
★ black construction paper
★ pencil or dark-colored chalk
★ sharp pencil or nail
★ grown-up helper

NOTE: Adult help needed with
sharp pencil or nail.

1. On the construction paper, draw a picture of someone or something important to you.

2. Get a grown-up to make small "star" holes in your drawing.

3. If you drew a person, poke holes in the shoulders, body, knees, hands, feet, and head. If you drew an animal, poke holes at the ends of its tail and nose, in its body, and at its feet. Don't make too many holes—make more than four, but not more than ten holes.

4. Hold the paper up to a bright light, or tape it to a window. The light shining through the holes will look like stars. This is your special constellation. All you have to do is name it!

create your own constellation

YOU'LL NEED:
* ★ tracing paper
* ★ pencils

One of the most famous constellations is Orion, the Hunter. It doesn't take a lot of imagination to see a hunter, holding his club over his head. But what else does that star picture look like?

1. Take a look at the stars of Orion on page 14 of this book. Lay your tracing paper over it and draw some big and small circles where the stars are.

2. Now, look at your paper and forget about Orion. What do you see when you look at the star pattern? Does it look like someone you know? Or something in your house, on your street, or in your city? Turn the paper around. Maybe it reminds you of a favorite TV show, movie, or book? Is it a butterfly, or a guitar?

3. Connect the brighter stars with lines to show what you see. Then finish by drawing a picture around them.

4. When you finish drawing your constellation, give it a name. You're doing what people have done for thousands of years—imagining pictures in the stars.

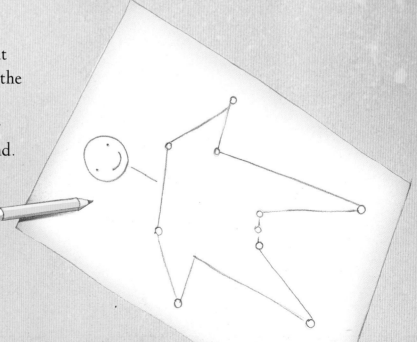

build a box full of stars

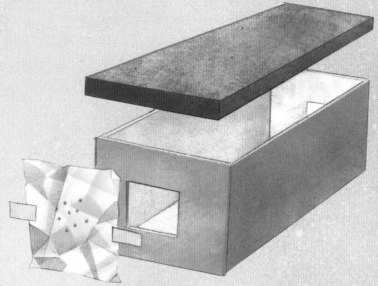

You'll need:
★ a small box (shoe box)
★ scissors
★ tracing paper
★ pencil
★ kitchen foil
★ pin
★ tape
★ grown-up helper

NOTE: Adult help needed with cutting of box and using pin or small nail.

Here's a star box you can make, with the help of a grown-up. Just follow these instructions:

1. Have your adult helper cut a 1-inch (2.5cm) hole in one end of the box. At the other end, cut out a hole about 3 inches (8cm) square.

2. Next, place some tracing paper over a constellation in the sky map—at the front and back of this book. With a pencil, carefully mark the positions of the main stars.

3. Place the paper over a section of foil—4 to 5 inches (10 to 12cm) square is a good size. Ask your helper to use the pin to poke holes where you have marked the stars, through both the paper and the foil.

4. Now, tape the foil over the larger hole in your box. The foil should cover the hole completely.

5. The star box is ready for you to use! Look into the box through the smaller hole. Point the box toward a bright lamp, so the light shines through the pinholes. You should see the constellation shining inside the box. Move the box around slowly. Do you see your pinhole stars twinkling?

Prepare more constellations for helpers to "pin" for your star box. They can make larger holes for the bright stars and smaller holes for the dim stars. This will make your miniature constellation look even more real.

47

INDEX

ABOUT THE AUTHOR

Chris Sasaki's love of astronomy began in grade school when he started reading science fiction, watching television coverage of Apollo astronauts landing on the moon, and looking at the stars and planets through a telescope in his backyard. At the McLaughlin Planetarium of the Royal Ontario Museum in Toronto, he wrote public astronomy shows and photographed astronomical sites around the world, including radio telescopes in New Mexico, astronomical observatories in northern Chile, the Space Shuttle at Cape Canaveral, and Mayan ruins in Mexico.

Chris teaches astronomy in public schools and in children's workshops, and writes for science magazines. He lives in Toronto.

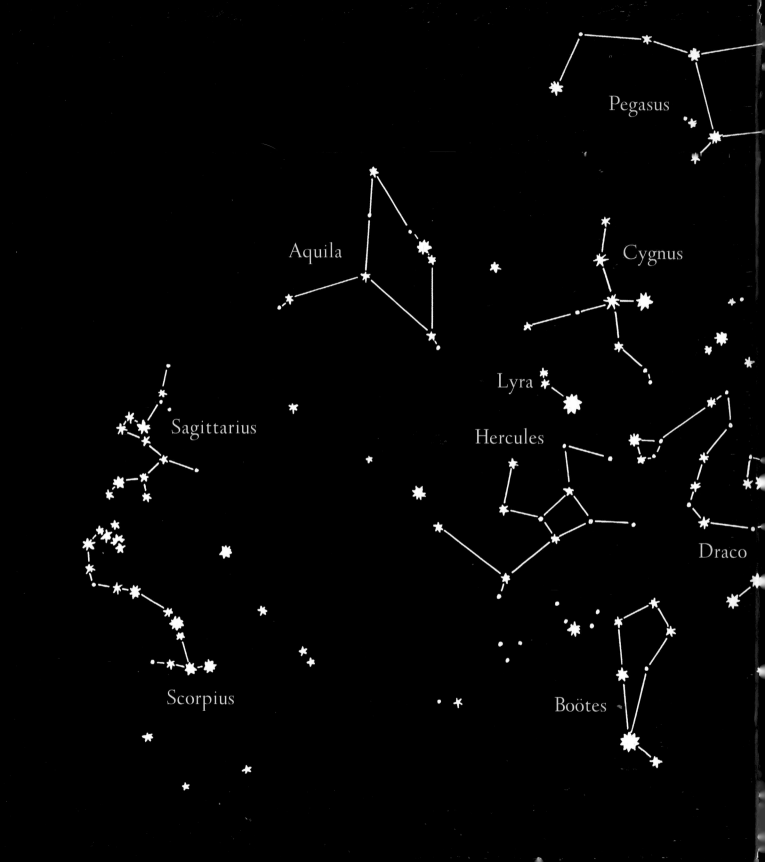